Cleo's Lost Ball

by Leslie McGuire

Illustrated by Carolyn Bracken and Sandrina Kurtz

Based on the books by Norman Bridwell

SCHOLASTIC INC.
New York Toronto London Auckland Sydney
Mexico City New Delhi Hong Kong Buenos Aires

"Is my ball here?" Cleo asks.

"No," says Clifford. "Why do you ask?"

"Because I lost it," says Cleo, "and I do not have another one."

"I will help you find it," says Clifford.

They went to the wall.

Clifford saw a large ball.

He hit it with his paws.

"Is this it?" he says.

"No," says Cleo. "That is another one because my ball is small."

Then they saw T-Bone.

"Come here and help us," says Cleo.

T-Bone and Cleo went down the hall.

"Here is a small ball," says T-Bone.

He held it in his jaws.

"That is not mine because it is too small," says Cleo.

T-Bone says, "I will crawl under here."

All he saw was another large ball.

"Why is Cleo so sad?" says Mac.

"Because her ball is lost," says Clifford.

Then Clifford saw a large shawl.

He went to look under it.

"Another small ball is under here!" he says.

"That is my ball!"
says Cleo.

It was not too large, and
not too small.

The dogs now had a
lot of balls.

So they all had a
great ball game.